The Shaking Continues

Who Will be Able to Endure the Coming Persecution and the Great Tribulation?

Charles Pretlow

The Shaking Continues
Who Will be Able to Endure the Coming Persecution and the Great Tribulation?
November 2023

Unless otherwise indicated, all Scripture quotations are from the Holy Bible, English Standard Version ® (ESV®), copyright © 2001 by Crossway, a publishing ministry of Good Publishers. Used with permission. All rights reserved.

ISBN 978-1-943412-25-9

Published by
Wilderness Voice Publishing
PO Box 857
Canon City, CO 81215
www.mcgmin.com

"A voice crying in the wilderness –
proclaiming the good news of the coming Kingdom!"

Contents

Birth Pains of the Coming Kingdom

Wars, Earthquakes, Pandemics, Corruption, Lawlessness and Mass Shootings, Sodom-like Perversion, Pre-flood Party Spirit, The Wicked Given Over to Debased Minds, Persecution and Slaughter of Jews, Persecution of True Christians, Signs in the Heavens, Continued Failure of Righteous Restoration— *the shaking continues with increased frequency and intensity*.

Jesus explained exactly how the end of this age events would unfold and right now those words of His should be resonating with every Christian. But sadly, few mainline Christians know and embrace enough of these words to wake up to the hour and become prepared to endure the final dark days we are now in.

In our online blog published in August 2023, we stated: "We are in another lull before the next big shaking" and indeed, the war in Israel starting in October 2023 with the worst atrocities against Jews since

Hitler's holocaust. This is another end of the age major shake-up, and Christ's predictions as recorded in Scripture are falling into place, one after another. His words about the end time are given to help awaken God's people. He said, *"And what I say to you I say to all: Stay awake"* (Mark 13:37).

Even on the day that I was tightening this message for our online blog version, the people in Maine are absolutely terrified as the hunt goes on for a mass shooter. Earlier in the week he went on a rampage and slaughtered 18 people and wounded 13 more. People in the region started clinging to their personal weapons, dusting off their Bibles, and praying.

We are in another round of satanic shaking allowed by God to wake up as many as possible, that they may get ready in time. The frequency and intensity of these shakings are increasing, inching towards severe trouble, chaos, economic calamity and nearing the complete breakdown of law and order.

<u>Racing Towards Armageddon</u>

This current shaking, the war by Hamas against Israel is stirring up a great division among the peoples and governments of the world. This situation can easily get out of hand and encompass all the enemies of Israel to launch another all-out attempt to annihilate the nation of Israel, igniting world war three.

It is Christian based nations siding with Israel holding back the tide. We must understand, protests around the world and in America (that side with the October 7th massacre of Jews) is a giant leap for Satan in building a worldwide consensus to destroy Israel. One of Satan's next major steps towards Armageddon is to finally sideline America and true Christianity.

Expect unrestrained persecution to increase against conservatives and true Christianity and a giant uptick in satanic attacks upon the serious disciple of Christ. Mark it down, persecution for being a believer in Christ is ramping up—get ready.

The Final Awakening and Harvest

The coming persecution for Christians will be used by God to purify the body of Christ (more on this later). Christ will have a cadre of solid disciples to bring forth the good news of the coming kingdom, just as the Great Tribulation ignites.

There are two final harvests about to take place, 1) the gathering of a multitude into eternity, 2) the bundling of the wicked for the nether gloom (hell).

The Great Tribulation will be the final awakening and harvest time: *"After this I looked, and behold, a <u>great multitude</u> that no one could number, from every nation, from all tribes and peoples and languages, standing before the throne and before the Lamb, clothed in white robes, with palm branches in their hands, and crying out with a loud voice, 'Salvation belongs to our God who sits on the throne, and to the*

7

*Lamb!' And all the angels were standing
around the throne and around the elders
and the four living creatures, and they fell
on their faces before the throne and
worshiped God"* (Revelation 7:9-11).

This vision of the final harvest of saved
souls was given to the Apostle John by an
angel of the Lord. In that revelation from
God, John learned who the multitudes are:
*"These are the ones coming out of <u>the great
tribulation.</u> They have washed their robes
and made them white in the blood of the
Lamb"* (Revelation 7:14).

Multitudes in the Valley of Decision

During the Great Tribulation phase,
Scriptures foretells that a multitude will
be in the valley of decision. The choice to
make for the unprepared will be between;
following the world masses brainwashed
to embrace the global unity and the
antichrist as savior of the world, or the
good news from the Lord's messengers
about the soon to come kingdom of God.

Clearing Up Christian Misinformation

False teachings that encourage the common believer in Christ to believe they'll never see trouble has blinded their prophetic insight. The main lies swallowed by far too many believers are:

- Christ will rapture Christians before the Great Tribulation.
- America was founded on Christian principles and will be exempt from persecution and end-time troubles.
- America's Christians will convert the world to Christianity, thus usher in Christ's return.
- Another foolish belief is that we will have another fifty years before any final end-time trouble begins.
- Another misunderstanding of the true end-time setting is that the Great Tribulation and the wrath of God both occur at the same time.

Scripture states that the wrath of God falls upon the world after the Great Tribulation (which is Satan's end-

9

time wrath,) and that time (the Great Tribulation) will be cut short by the rescue of the saints (commonly known as the rapture).

Thus, Christians must be ready to endure massive persecution, and a good portion of the Great Tribulation, but be rescued just as the wrath of God befalls the world. *"For then there will be great tribulation, such as has not been from the beginning of the world until now, no, and never will be. And if those days had not been cut short, no human being would be saved. But for the <u>sake of the elect those days will be cut short</u>"* (Matthew 24:21-22).

As for the rescue of God's elect (true Christians) commonly known as the rapture. Here Scripture is clear when the rapture will take place: *"But in those days, after that tribulation, the sun will be darkened, and the moon will not give its light, and the stars will be falling from heaven, and the powers in the heavens will be shaken. And then they will see the*

Son of Man coming in clouds with great power and glory. And then he will send out the angels and gather his elect from the four winds, from the ends of the earth to the ends of heaven" (Mark 13:24-27).

Christian Sanctification

Instant transformation when born-again is another outrageous lie. Being told that one is swept into eternal security when initially born again has caused a multitude of believers to be unprepared to endure to the end. Many, many are at risk of losing their salvation due to lack of understanding concerning sanctification that is required by all believers in Christ.

The Apostle Peter wrote: *"Like newborn infants, long for the pure spiritual milk, that by it you may grow up into salvation— if indeed you have tasted that the Lord is good"* (1 Peter 2:2-3).

Few believers are instructed on how to grow up into salvation, which is the process of sanctification in where a new believer works out their salvation in fear and trembling (as the Apostle Paul put it).

Sanctification is to be embraced in the discipline of the Lord with an end goal of obtaining the grace of God, crucifying all the works of the old nature, with its passions and desires.

When a born-again believer matures in sanctification, Christlike character is formed within. Sanctification is the process of putting off one's old nature that still remains after becoming born again, and within that process, with the power of God we put on a nature that is Christlike.

Sanctification leads us to obtain the grace of God and live on Earth with eternal security and never to lose faith (salvation), even onto death.

The sincere believer while working out his or her salvation is under the grace of God and his loving hand of discipline. This protection of safety and grace while on the journey to sanctification can be lost if, while in process we stray away from Christ and fall back into sinning deliberately. *"For if we go on sinning deliberately after receiving the knowledge of the truth, there no longer remains a sacrifice for sins, but a fearful expectation of judgment, and a fury of fire that will consume the adversaries"* (Hebrews 10:26-27).

The real issue for Christians has become; are you as a believer in Christ ready to endure what has already started, to endure severe persecution and the Great Tribulation and stand before Christ at his appearance?

Many godly Christians will be imprisoned and even martyred. And many who are unprepared will fall away.

How to Get Ready?
For years, since 1998 our ministry has been warning Christians that the end-time troubles have started and how to get ready.

So far, few mainline Christians want to hear the truth, and even fewer act upon the truth if they choose to listen. Our first book on the subject was published in 2004.

There had been many messages given and books written prior by other ministries and authors, but few warned believers that they would have to endure severe persecution and a large part of the Great Tribulation before Christ returns. And with those few warnings, very little instruction was given on how to endure and survive the coming troubles that Christians will be required to suffer.

Persecution and Lawlessness that Cleans House

With Hamas attacking Israel, and Israel responding, horrific persecution has increasingly risen against the Jewish people and Israel worldwide. Christians need to understand that persecution against Israel will rapidly envelope Christianity, on a large scale, especially in

America. (Primarily, because most Christians stand with Israel.)

This coming persecution will keep sputtering on and off but will eventually gain intense hatred towards Christians along with the Jews. Soon, many lukewarm believers will fall away and even betray other Christians in the coming days—just as Christ explained: *"Then they will deliver you up to tribulation and put you to death, and you will be hated by all nations for my name's sake. And then many will fall away and betray one another and hate one another"* (Matthew 24:9-10).

Nothing seems to turn the tide against the political and cultural oppression towards restoration of cultural righteousness and morality. Satan has stolen control of just about every sacred institution that steered the American culture towards civility and morality. Chaos and corruption in politics, education, church, the military— it seems that every pinnacle of American success is mysteriously crumbling. Indeed, this is the last days' work of Satan.

The Apostle Paul framed these current end-time chaotic events as follows: *"For the mystery of lawlessness is already at work. Only he who now restrains it will do so until he is out of the way. And then the lawless one will be revealed, whom the Lord Jesus will kill with the breath of his mouth and bring to nothing by the appearance of his coming. The coming of the lawless one is by the <u>activity of Satan</u> with all power and false signs and wonders, and with all wicked deception for those who are perishing, because they refused to love the truth and so be saved. Therefore God sends them a <u>strong delusion</u>, so that they may believe what is false, in order that all may be condemned who did not believe the truth but had pleasure in unrighteousness"* (2 Thessalonians 2:7-12).

Today, we see multitudes given over to a strong delusion, to believe what is false, and act out lawlessness. The love of pleasure and sin has deceived the masses, hardened their hearts, and locked their minds into a strong delusion. (Forget challenging them with truth, if God has given up, how can we as Christians convert those who God gave up? See Romans 1:24-32.)

In the end, many Christians will find out that they also were given up by God because they preferred to believe lies and fooled themselves into thinking they were right with Christ. Jesus was very clear on this deadly condition that many Christians would be "bound up" in: *"Not everyone who says to me, 'Lord, Lord,' will enter the kingdom of heaven, but the one who does the will of my Father who is in heaven. On that day many will say to me, 'Lord, Lord, did we not prophesy in your name, and cast out demons in your name, and do many mighty works in your name?' And then will I declare to them, 'I never knew you; depart from me, you workers of lawlessness'"* (Matthew 7:21-23).

Many Christians attend church faithfully and are religious in their behavior. And many Charismatic and Pentecostal Christians practice the gifts, prophesying and casting out demons. Unfortunately, far too many of these believers are working for Jesus, in name only. They have religion, but do not have a true relationship with Christ. They work tirelessly for Jesus in their own strength, but Jesus is not working through them. *"And then will I declare to them, 'I never knew you!'"*

The last days persecution of Christians will be allowed by God, and there will be no way to avoid these coming attacks that are hate filled, unless one gives up their faith in Christ. The Apostle Paul's words ring out about persecution: *"Indeed, all who desire to live a godly life in Christ Jesus will be persecuted, while evil people and impostors will go on from bad to worse, deceiving and being deceived"* (2 Timothy 3:12-13).

The sincere believer who becomes prepared, having a solid godly relationship with Christ will suffer persecution and some trouble, but will be able to endure the persecution, stand firm, and in the end be victorious at Christ's appearance—however some will be imprisoned and martyred.

Believe it or not, persecution will be used by the Lord to wake up and clean up his Church. Christ will have a purified Church distinctive from all other forms of Christianity. Christ's Church, the true body of Christ will walk in beauty, purity, perfection, and great spiritual power. This coming end-time Church will not be under the auspices of any one denomination or group of denominations, or any special leader(s).

Christ is very serious when he said he will have a purified Church at the end: *"The Son of Man will send his angels, and they will gather out of his kingdom all causes of sin and all law-breakers, and throw them*

*into the fiery furnace. In that place there
will be weeping and gnashing of teeth.
Then the righteous will shine like the sun in
the kingdom of their Father. He who has
ears, let him hear"* (Matthew 13:41-43).

Christians Struggling With a Seared Conscience, Over Confidence in Self, and Secret Sin

Many sincere believers living in our
corrupt American culture suffer from
past defilements and harbor carnal
character structures. These inner old
nature traits invite temptations and give
the devil a free hand.

In addition, many believers lack the fear of
God because they trust in themselves
rather than God. Many on fire believers
are in denial of these hidden latent issues
and as the end unfolds, Satan will demand
to sift these carnal and lukewarm believers
in attempt to destroy their faith and drag
them into hell.

As you recall, Satan demanded to sift
Peter due to Peter's denial of having dual

personalities. Jesus intervened for Peter only to a point, praying that Peter's faith would not fail. Jesus allowed Peter to become publicly humiliated to a point.

Many Christians are about to suffer severe sifting by the devil, with no way of stopping the onslaught until they break denial of their reliance on self, their self-centeredness, and their secret sins—or fall away from Christ altogether.

Today, many believers are like Peter, unaware of their double-minded condition. Here is the passage to help embrace the fact that many Christians can be in denial of inner divided personalities that will allow them to be sifted by the devil: *"'Simon, Simon, behold, Satan demanded to have <u>you</u>, that he might sift <u>you</u> like wheat, but I have prayed for <u>you</u> that your faith may not fail. And when you have turned again, strengthen your brothers.' Peter said to him, 'Lord, I am ready to go with you both to prison and to death.' Jesus said, 'I tell you, Peter, the* *rooster will not crow this day, until you deny three times that you know me'"* (Luke 22:31-34). **Please note** I have underlined three words in this passage. In the original language the first two uses, Christ used a word that denotes both of you, "*to have [both of] you, that he might sift [both of] you*". Whereas the last use in this passage Christ used the word that denotes just one of you, *"but I have prayed for [one of] you that your faith may not fail."*

Peter was confident in his own ability to follow Christ, no matter what, even unto death. However, Christ saw a flaw in Peter's character that weakened his faith and told Peter that he would deny knowing him three times. Later, when this prediction of Christ's came to pass Peter's denial began to break. Then after Christ's resurrection our Lord appeared to Peter and confronted Peter on his love towards the things on Earth, more than his love towards Christ.

Through Peter's persecution and testing, Peter was awakened to the truth about his faith. At that point Christ was able to confront Peter on his hidden issues of heart and dividedness, which was how Peter loved the things on Earth, much more than he loved Christ. Peter struggled years later with his dividedness in where the Apostle Paul had to confront him again. (See Galatians 2:11-14.)

This is another reason why so many Christians are not awake and are at risk, they love and worry about life in this age and the things of this world much more than they love God and many ignorantly suffer from a doubleminded condition (multiple personalities).

Some who follow our ministry believe we should lighten up and not be so harsh concerning what we see coming and how so many believers are in a poor relationship with the Lord. Unfortunately, for years and years, God's people have been soothed into thinking that they are right with God, safe and protected, when in fact many are at risk of being rejected by the Lord.

Our own persecution from other believers is a small price to pay to inform God's people what they need to hear. The Apostle Paul predicted that many would stop up their ears: *"For the time is coming when people will not endure sound teaching, but having itching ears they will accumulate for themselves teachers to suit their own passions, and will turn away from listening to the truth and wander off into myths"* (2 Timothy 4:3-4).

A Seared Conscience: Through the many years of ministry and pastoral counseling, a common theme of hardness of heart and bitterness became obvious. These struggling Christians loved God but had an underlining beef with God because of their past wounding abuses in childhood. Most formed an "I'm a Victim" inner stance and mentality.

Often, their abuse towards others, even towards their own children, was minimized, rationalized, and justified, as they learned to push their sins far from their conscience. (Review 1 Timothy 1:18-20.)

The Apostle Paul wrote to wage good warfare and by: *"holding faith and a good conscience. By rejecting this, some have made shipwreck of their faith, among whom are Hymenaeus and Alexander, whom I have handed over to Satan that they may learn not to blaspheme"* (1 Timothy 1:19-20).

These people have rejected the pain of conscience when sinning and doing evil. They then suffer wrong for wrongdoing but deny any responsibility and eventually try to become a Christian in the hope of a better life on Earth and eternal life in heaven. They come to Christ but are never taught to deal with their inner hardened heart, seared conscience and inner self-pity stance that lends to bitter jealousy and selfish ambition. Thus, they are easily used by Satan within relationships and fellowships to cause devilish problems.

These people, after coming to Christ formed an outer righteousness and easily see and point out the sins of others and complain, but as for their own selfish attitudes and sinful actions, they were blind. *"But these, like irrational animals, creatures of instinct, born to be caught and destroyed, blaspheming about matters of which they are ignorant, will also be destroyed in their destruction, suffering wrong as the wage for their wrongdoing. They count it pleasure to revel in the daytime. They are blots and blemishes, reveling in their deceptions, while they feast with you. They have eyes full of adultery, insatiable for sin. They entice unsteady souls. They have hearts trained in greed. Accursed children!"* (2 Peter 2:12-14).

Reliance on Self-Righteousness: Then there are seemingly stalwart believers who walk in righteousness, convinced they are protected and blessed by God due to their righteousness.

Unfortunately, these believers are at risk of severe attacks from the devil during these last days. Like Job, they cannot see their own inner picture of self-reliance upon their own righteousness and self-inner strength.

When trouble came by the hand of the devil, Job justified his self above God and blamed God for what Satan had done to him. When one is in a self-righteous inner stance, Satan has a right to bring extra evil into one's life. (Study the book of Job without other commentator's misinterpretation.) You will find Job's real issue is simply explained in this passage: *"So these three men ceased to answer Job, because he was <u>righteous in his own eyes</u>. Then Elihu the son of Barachel the Buzite, of the family of Ram, burned with anger. He burned with anger at Job because <u>he justified himself rather than God</u>"* (Job 32:1-2).

Many Christians are righteous in their own eyes and live as having an "I'm better than that sinner" attitude and justify, rationalize, and minimize their inner self-righteous heart. When Job was finally confronted by Elihu about his condition, Job then was able to finally hear the voice of God. The Lord's discourse was very similar to Elihu's confrontation of Job. Finally, brokenness came upon Job, which led Job to the following understanding: *"I had heard of you by the hearing of the ear, but now my eye sees you; therefore I despise myself, and repent in dust and ashes"* (Job 42:5-6).

Every believer sooner than later will need to see their own righteousness as filthy rags and definitely come to the true understanding of their (and everyone's) wretchedness. Because so many ministries and pastors make coming to Jesus like buying life insurance, few so-called born-again believers ever truly see their own wickedness and repent with a proper attitude of heart. Nor do they continue on in the discipline of the Lord, becoming sanctified, growing up in salvation and eternal security. Christians must be on guard from falling into the trap of building a religious relationship with God. This creates a dynamic of lies and a false sense of belonging to God. Study the Apostle Paul's account of his coming to understand his own dire condition of self. This realization came upon Paul after he became a believer in Christ.

Paul's words will ring-out for many Christians in the coming days when persecution and trouble come in like a flood. By God's grace may all see their love for life on Earth and their self-righteousness melt and realize their tremendous need for Jesus and His righteousness: *"Wretched man that I am! Who will deliver me from this body of death? Thanks be to God through Jesus Christ our Lord!"* (Romans 7:24-25).

Secret Sin Christians: Christians who sin deliberately and hide their sinful activity usually start out struggling against their pet sin but end up giving in to it readily. When sinning deliberately, then judgement looms and eventually they are exposed publicly. *"For if we go on sinning deliberately after receiving the knowledge of the truth, there no longer remains a sacrifice for sins, but a fearful expectation of judgment, and a fury of fire that will consume the adversaries"* (Hebrews 10:26-27).

The key is confession with goldy grief and turning away from secret sins. *"Therefore, confess your sins to one another and pray for one another, that you may be healed"* (James 5:16).

Grace, Forgiveness and Accountability

When we are overtaken by any sin and admit it, confess, and seek forgiveness from God and those we affend, we should not condemn ourselves. In helping others who are overtaken: *"Brothers, if anyone is caught in any transgression, you who are spiritual should restore him in a spirit of gentleness. Keep watch on yourself, lest you too be tempted. Bear one another's burdens, and so fulfill the law of Christ"* (Galatians 6:1-2).

God holds all accountable. It is important to remember, as believers we will reap extra trouble when we sin, regardless of being overtaken by sin, or sinning deliberately: *"Do not be deceived: God is not mocked, for whatever one sows, that will he also reap. For the one who sows to his own flesh will from the flesh reap corruption, but the one who sows to the Spirit will from the Spirit reap eternal life"* (Galatians 6:7-8).

Godly Grief that Leads to True Repentance and Salvation

The lukewarm believer in Christ, the "secret sin" Christian, and the self-righteous follower of Christ, all are at great risk of losing their eternal salvation.

Again, the teaching that says that once one is born-again, they cannot lose their salvation is another lie that has caused many Christians to live a carnal self-centered life, often causing them to become overtaken with sin. Scripture states that we are to grow up into salvation, obtain the grace of God, humbly walk in holiness, overcoming the sin nature by putting to death the passions and desires of the flesh.

When we choose to follow the path to a real relationship with God, Jesus warns that it will be hard. We will make mistakes, sometimes become overtaken by a sin, or often become discouraged. Satan and evil at times will come out of the woodwork.

The key to obtaining the grace of God as a believer is to continue on, and deal (not ignore) each old carnal nature issue that crops up and stands in the way. Suppressing the passions and desires of the flesh is foolish and religious, however, learning to work with the Holy Spirit to bring death to the root issues of the flesh is vital and facilitates the resurrected life in Christ.

When we die to these internal issues, then when temptations come to arouse a carnal desire, we rest safely in the Lord. Because the root issues have been brought to death and replaced by Christlike character and the Holy Spirit enables the resurrected life in Christ and eternal security: *"And those who belong to Christ Jesus have crucified the flesh with its passions and desires"* (Galatians 5:24).

As we become mature in Christ, walking in his discipline, we will learn how to stand against the powers of darkness. Sometimes this will demand intense spiritual warfare lasting for quite some time.

A proper beginning on this journey of growing up in salvation is dealing properly with one's own hidden issues of heart. By having the proper attitude of heart like Job obtained, we will come to a point of despising our own carnal self and repent with godly grief. *"For godly grief produces a repentance that leads to salvation without regret, whereas worldly grief produces death"* (2 Corinthians 7:10).

Giving the Lord permission to bring testing into our lives is another aspect of growing up into salvation. It is through the discipline of the Lord and bitter battles with the devil that affords obtaining the grace of God, where we walk in the Lord's holiness, resting from our own self-righteous energy and efforts.

In the book of James, the author capsulizes this journey by writing: *"Blessed is the man who remains steadfast under trial, for when he has stood the test he will receive the crown of life, which God has promised to those who love him. Let no one say when he is tempted, 'I am being tempted by God,' for God cannot be tempted with evil, and he himself tempts no one. But each person is tempted when he is lured and enticed by his own desire. Then desire when it has conceived gives birth to sin,*

34

and sin when it is fully grown brings forth death" (James 1:12-15).

We can stockpile food, water, fuel and have a secret hideout, thinking to ride out the coming Great Tribulation and antichrist rule. Don't fool ourselves, the only way to navigate through the coming trouble is by having a true relationship with Christ, that is instilled, trained, and disciplined into us by His hand. By obtaining this true relationship with Christ, He will lead and provide for us every step of the way, which may include stockpiling food, water, fuel, and a place to hide. This pathway through the coming troubles is by abiding in Christ and walking in true holiness: *"And a highway shall be there, and it shall be called the Way of Holiness; the unclean shall not pass over it. It shall belong to those who walk on the way; even if they are fools, they shall not go astray"* (Isaiah 35:8).

There is Still Time to
Embrace Christ's Discipline

"Do not love the world or the things in the world. If anyone loves the world, the love of the Father is not in him. For all that is in the world—the desires of the flesh and the desires of the eyes and pride of life—is not from the Father but is from the world. And the world is passing away along with its desires, but whoever does the will of God abides forever" (1 John 2:15-17).

In following Christ, it requires dying to the **desires of the flesh**, the **desires of the eyes**, and the **pride of life.** The discipline of the Lord will primarily focus on these three aspects of our old carnal nature. In the days to come, these are the areas of life a carnal Christian will be forced to deal with, for they will be attacked by Satan. Satan will demand every sincere believer in Christ to be challenged with their love towards God versus the love of this world.

Desires of the Flesh: These are things that we lust after and we can afford to obtain,

36

to fulfill idolatrous desires. Obsessive activities such as physical strength and physical looks, ownership of material possessions, relationship ownership, in general unhealthy and sinful desires: sexual immorality, impurity, sensuality, idolatry, sorcery, enmity, strife, jealousy, fits of anger, rivalries, dissensions, divisions, envy, drunkenness, orgies. The Apostle Paul warns: *"I warn you, as I warned you before, that those who do such things will not inherit the kingdom of God"* (Galatians 5:21).

Desires of the Eyes: These are the sinful desires to possess what we see or to have those things which have visual appeal. The coveting of money, possessions, or other physical things is not from God, but from the world around us. Lusting after the things we see, but can't possess ignites envy, jealousy, and selfishness. This leads to manipulating and gaslighting people to gain advantage and relationship dominance.

Pride of Life: Christ said: *"For everyone who exalts himself will be humbled, and he who humbles himself will be exalted."* (Luke 14:11). We can pride ourselves on many things. The pride of life describes an arrogant spirit of self-sufficiency. We can become religiously prideful. Pride expresses the desire for recognition, applause, status, and advantage in life.

Christians who have been wounded in the past, especially in childhood generally feel insecure and unimportant. These inner feelings are counterbalanced by developing a hardened heart and an inner comparison mechanism that looks for faults in others and elevates oneself by overemphasizing any self-success.

Brokenness that Restores the Joy of Salvation

In these coming dark turbulent days, many will suffer financial loss, relationship troubles, and overwhelming demonic spiritual oppression. As the end-time troubles become more extreme, most unprepared Christians will be just like the masses in the world—full of fear and hysteria, just as Christ said: *"People fainting with fear and with foreboding of what is coming on the world. For the powers of the heavens will be shaken"* (Luke 21:26).

These troubles and trials are meant to break the hardened hearts of lukewarm Christians and lost sinners. A reaping is coming for all of God's people who are not ready, which God is allowing to wake up the unprepared.

Psalm 51 will be key for many in the coming days when their denial is broken, as their secret heart issues are brought to light. David wrote the following after he was confronted with his secret sin by the prophet: *"Behold, you delight in truth in the inward being, and you teach me wisdom in the secret heart"* (Psalm 51:6).

Later on, in Psalm 51 David expresses an important principle of true godly grief, brokenness and repentance: *"The sacrifices of God are a broken spirit; a broken and contrite heart, O God, you will not despise"* (Psalm 51:17).

Dear Christian, are you bound up by the cares of this life, feeling distant from the presence of the Lord within you? Is fear of what is coming upon the world controlling you? Repent, turn with all your heart back to the Lord, and He will restore the joy of your salvation. You will learn to straighten up, raise your head in preparation and hope to greet Christ at his appearance.

Give up on the world and don't look back. Live as if you were exiled in a foreign hostile land. For Jesus said that when these last day events take place, know that your redemption is drawing near. Be ready to leave this world, your homes, vehicles, unsaved loved ones, your occupation.

Satan is about to be cast out of heavens and thrown down to the Earth as he loses the battle in the heaven. He has had great influence upon the Earth since the fall of Adam and Eve—developing evil people to take over. Satan's final place of resistance will be the Earth. *"Therefore, rejoice, O heavens and you who dwell in them! But woe to you, O earth and sea, for the devil has come down to you in great wrath, because he knows that his time is short!"* (Revelation 12:12).

The devil will setup rulership of the world through the antichrist—temporarily. Let the wicked have it, when Christ physically returns, we get all back when he sets his feet on Earth and establishes his 1,000-year reign in Jerusalem.

Very little time is left to prepare oneself. Jesus warned: *"But stay awake at all times, praying that you may have strength to escape all these things that are going to take place, and to stand before the Son of Man"* (Luke 21:36). We need to strengthen our faith in Christ by his loving hand that disciplines, trains, and transforms.

The Midnight Cry

One last thing to consider. Jesus gave a parable concerning the general condition of his followers at the darkest hour of humanity. That condition would be that most Christians would be sound asleep as they waited for the return of Christ. (See Matthew 25:1-13.)

In the parable, Jesus used the story of ten virgins waiting for the bride groom. Five of the maidens were wise and carried extra oil so they could trim their lamps if the wait was too long, into the midnight hour. The other five maidens, Jesus identified them as foolish, because they did not bring extra oil.

Then at midnight the bridegroom sent out his closest servants to cry out and declare: *"Here is the bridegroom! Come out to meet him.' Then all those virgins rose and trimmed their lamps"* (Matthew 25:6-7).

The five foolish virgins did not have enough oil to trim their lamps to see clearly at the cry that came at midnight as they waited for the bridegroom to finally appear. They begged the wise virgins for some of their extra oil but were turned down, so they went to the dealers to buy extra oil and left their place where they were to meet the bridegroom.

While the five foolish virgins were away, the bridegroom came, and five wise virgins were ready waiting and left to enter into the home of the bridegroom.

Then, when the five foolish virgins returned and found that they were left behind. They all came to the bridegroom's home and knocked on his door to let them in.

Here is the terrible warning for all Christian in this hour from the parable of the Ten Virgins: *"Afterward the other virgins came also, saying, 'Lord, lord, open to us.' But he answered, 'Truly, I say to you, I do not know you.' Watch therefore, for you know neither the day nor the hour"* (Matthew 25:11-13).

Many carnal unprepared Christians will be locked out and left behind on that glorious day!

We encourage you to take to heart what we have shared in this little book. Through our own trials and battles we attest to the faithfulness of Christ when we allow him to discipline us to become his true servants. As the Apostle Paul instructs, we must do the following: *"Work out your own salvation with fear and trembling, for it is God who works in you, both to will and to work for his good pleasure"* (Philippians 2:12-13).

Which is Your Eternal Destiny?

Soon, a great multitude of people worldwide will be thrust into making a decision that will determine their eternal destiny. The choice will be, go along with the antichrist's promises of prosperity and peace or turn to the Gospel of Christ and hold out for his appearance and eventual physical return.

The antichrist's pitch will be backed by a supernatural being (the 2nd beast of Revelation), that will demonstrate signs and wonders and even cause fire to come down from the sky.

But the antichrist won't be a typical political leader but be declared a god to be worshipped and obeyed. His plan to bring utopia to the world will require absolute conformity to his rulership and a system for controlling the masses by a network monitoring system.

This system will require some kind of incision with an implant that connects every human being into a global cloud database. In the book of Revelation, the Apostle John describes this system that is forced upon everyone as taking a mark (incision) indicated by the number 666.

Jesus said the rise of the antichrist would come during the Great Tribulation and the deception would be powerful and wonderous. *"For false christs and false prophets will arise and perform great signs and wonders, so as to lead astray, if possible, even the elect"* (Matthew 24:24).

On the other hand, the Lord's servants will continue to proclaim the only real good news. Jesus said of that time leading into the Great Tribulation when the antichrist appears: *"And this gospel of the kingdom will be proclaimed throughout the whole world as a testimony to all nations, and then the end will come.* (Matthew 24:14).

Utopia on Earth (a lie) or the gospel (good news) of the coming kingdom of heaven. Everyone worldwide, from the lost sinner to the seasoned saint will be forced to make a choice—very soon.

Making the wrong choice by taking the mark and buying into the antichrist's governing system will drag us into hell. Then, at the end of Christ's 1,000 reign on Earth, the final judgment comes where all the residence of hell, the fallen angels, demons, the antichrist, and 2nd beast will be cast in the lake of fire as described in the book of Revelation.

Jesus referred to the lake of fire as the second death. A divinely created "spirit incinerator" that destroys sin, hell itself with all residing therein, the antichrist, Satan and his minions. *"Then Death and Hades were thrown into the lake of fire. This is the second death, the lake of fire. And if anyone's name was not found written in the book of life, he was thrown into the lake of fire"* (Revelation 20:14-15).

Those who hold out as believers, the masses who call on the name Christ will enter into eternal life where it is stated in Scripture: *Behold, the dwelling place of God is with man. He will dwell with them, and they will be his people, and God himself will be with them as their God"* (Revelation 21:3).

Find and Attend a Fellowship that Will Help Equip You

My hope is that this message has stirred and inspired you to give yourself to the discipline of the Lord, that he may guide you and train you, sanctify and prepare you. We recommend that you find solid like-minded fellowship and get connected with like-minded believers. If you are not a believer, I encourage you to seek Christ, turn away from sin, and become a believer and a member of God's army, learning to be equipped for life and ministry in these last days. Keep in mind, as a new believer you must learn to embrace the Lord's discipline and inner character transformation, so as to grow up into salvation.

Soon, many will want to hear how to become ready, so it is important that the sincere Christian become effective in sharing the gospel (good news) of the coming kingdom.

Contact Information

You can contact the author by the following:

Mail: MC Global Ministries
Charles Pretlow
PO Box 857
Canon City, CO 81215

Phone: (719) 285-8542

Email: contact@mcgmin.com

Website: www.mcgmin.com

If this message helps, please consider helping us: Your donations to support this work are most appreciated: Donate today by mail or online by using our secure website with the above contact information. Thank you!

Guest Speaker

Charles is available as a guest speaker. His extensive background in ministry, counseling, and end-of-this-age issues provides sound instruction on overcoming the last-days troubles and wounds to the personal spirit and damaged emotions.

More About the Author

Pastor Charles Pretlow began his ministerial work in 1974 and shares insights gained from years of study, ministry, and counseling Christians who struggled in their walk with Christ. He shares sound teachings to help equip the sincere Christian and those in leadership to effectively minister in these dark days leading to Christ's return. Charles' theology is practical, founded in years of experience and his own recovery from a wounded spirit and damaged emotions. His training in the discipline of the Lord has taught him to rely—not on himself, but on the Holy Spirit and Christ's leadership.

www.ingramcontent.com/pod-product-compliance
Lightning Source LLC
Chambersburg PA
CBHW071437040426
42445CB00012BA/1385